Classic Fretwork Scroll Saw Patterns

Patrick Spielman & James Reidle

Art by Dirk Boelman, The Art Factory

 Sterling Publishing Co., Inc.   New York

Library of Congress Cataloging-in-Publication Data

Spielman, Patrick.
    Classic fretwork scroll saw patterns / by Patrick Spielman & James
Reidle : art by Dirk Boelman.
       p.   cm.
    Includes index.
    ISBN 0-8069-8254-3
    1. Fretwork. 2. Jig saws. I. Reidle, James. II. Title.
TT186.S665   1991
745'.51—dc20   90-29137
                                              CIP

Edited by Rodman Neumann

10 9 8 7 6 5 4 3 2 1

© 1991 by Patrick Spielman and James Reidle
Published by Sterling Publishing Company, Inc.
387 Park Avenue South, New York, N.Y. 10016
Distributed in Canada by Sterling Publishing
% Canadian Manda Group, P.O. Box 920, Station U
Toronto, Ontario, Canada M8Z 5P9
Distributed in Great Britain and Europe by Cassell PLC
Villiers House, 41/47 Strand, London WC2N 5JE, England
Distributed in Australia by Capricorn Ltd.
P.O. Box 665, Lane Cove, NSW 2066
Manufactured in the United States of America
All rights reserved

Sterling ISBN 0-8069-8254-3

Contents

Acknowledgments

We are especially grateful to Dirk Boelman of The Art Factory for his outstanding work in preparing the final art for each and every pattern. Scroll-sawyers are sure to appreciate Dirk's smooth, flowing lines and precision detailing.

Thank you, Sherri Spielman Valitchka, for shading some of the patterns. We also extend our gratitude to Jerry Spruiell of Memory Lane for permitting us to include two of his superb antique car patterns, and thanks to John Schreiner and Carl Weckhorst who were also helpful.

Patrick Spielman,
Spielmans Wood Works, and
James Reidle,
Reidle Products

Metric Conversion

INCHES TO MILLIMETRES AND CENTIMETRES

MM—millimetres   *CM—centimetres*

Inches	MM	CM	Inches	CM	Inches	CM
⅛	3	0.3	9	22.9	30	76.2
¼	6	0.6	10	25.4	31	78.7
⅜	10	1.0	11	27.9	32	81.3
½	13	1.3	12	30.5	33	83.8
⅝	16	1.6	13	33.0	34	86.4
¾	19	1.9	14	35.6	35	88.9
⅞	22	2.2	15	38.1	36	91.4
1	25	2.5	16	40.6	37	94.0
1¼	32	3.2	17	43.2	38	96.5
1½	38	3.8	18	45.7	39	99.1
1¾	44	4.4	19	48.3	40	101.6
2	51	5.1	20	50.8	41	104.1
2½	64	6.4	21	53.3	42	106.7
2	76	7.6	22	55.9	43	109.2
3½	89	8.9	23	58.4	44	111.8
4	102	10.2	24	61.0	45	114.3
4½	114	11.4	25	63.5	46	116.8
5	127	12.7	26	66.0	47	119.4
6	152	15.2	27	68.6	48	121.9
7	178	17.8	28	71.1	49	124.5
8	203	20.3	29	73.7	50	127.0

Introduction

Some of the highly detailed and ornate patterns in this book were originally created in the nineteenth century by early scroll-saw masters. Included here and blended with some of our own creations and derivations are designs published in the mid to late 1800s. Where necessary the old designs have been changed or altered to make them more adaptable to present-day scroll-sawing techniques (Illus. 1). These refinements were executed by Dirk Boelman, probably today's most talented and productive designer and developer of fine scroll-saw fretwork patterns.

Some of the larger project patterns extend across three to four or more adjoining pages. Some large symmetrical patterns are given just in half or quarter patterns. These are designated with dividing lines or lines of rotation where patterns should be folded or flipped and joined to form the complete, full pattern.

To conserve space, some of the more obvious pattern profiles have been eliminated, including rectangle patterns for box bottoms and liners, and shelves for wall brackets. Also omitted are half-circular and quarter-circular shaped patterns that comprise the wall shelf and/or corner shelves for various bracket projects.

Illus. 1 Fretwork is done with modern constant-tension scroll saws and new materials such as very thin plywoods that make it easier and faster than ever before possible.

Thicknesses, Materials, and Blade Sizes

Many of the older pattern designs given in the book were probably originally sawn from thin, solid woods 1/8- to 5/16-inch thick, depending upon the nature of the project. With today's modern scroll saws, thicker materials are much more easily cut. This option may make some of the projects, such as silhouettes and picture or mirror frames, more interesting. Wherever a certain thickness is required, it is specified directly on the pattern or in a caption. Otherwise, unless specified, any thickness can be used as dictated by your personal preference.

Because of the delicacy of some of the very ornate and fragile pieces, you may want to select plywood. It will always be easiest to finish-sand surfaces before sawing. A good constant-tension scroll saw should produce sawn surfaces that form the profile edges so smooth that they will not require subsequent sanding.

Many of the patterns are so detailed that they will require very small "saw gates" or blade entry holes that can only be threaded with fine pinless blades (Illus. 2). The most delicate cuttings will require a fine No. 2, 3, or 4 blade. Most patterns can be cut with medium blades (No.'s 5–7), and some of the larger projects should be cut with No. 8 to No. 11 blades. Always use the biggest possible blade, but do not sacrifice the ability to cut fine detail or the smoothness of the cut surface. Thicker materials will obviously require heavier blades, so plan accordingly.

Illus. 2   A close-up look at fine fret-sawing. The blade has been threaded through a small hole ("saw gate") drilled into the waste area. Here three pieces of thin plywood (1/8" or 3 mm) are being stack-sawn all at once to make identical pieces for the fan project given on page 61. A fine (No. 4) pinless blade is being used.

Developing and Transferring Patterns

One of the biggest problems with past scroll-sawing activities is developing patterns and transferring them to the workpiece. Since all patterns in this book are given in the recommended full-size versions, no enlargements or reductions are actually necessary unless some other special size is desired. The toy furniture patterns for example may be enlarged to accommodate a certain, special doll size. In such cases the easiest and quickest way to make size changes is with the assistance of an office copier that has enlarging and reducing capabilities. Otherwise, the old process of drawing grids or using a pantograph can be employed, but these methods are often time consuming and not very accurate.

Use the office copy machine to make an exact copy of the patterns you intend to saw. The copies can then be temporarily bonded directly onto the surface of the workpiece. Use a brush-on rubber cement or a temporary bonding spray adhesive (Illus. 3). We personally prefer the spray adhesive technique. Simply spray a very light mist of adhesive to the back of the pattern copy (**do not spray on wood**) and wait just a few seconds; then press the pattern onto the wood with your hand (Illus. 3). Saw out the piece following exactly the same lines of the pattern. This technique results in far more accurate finished cuts (with smoother curves, etc.). It also saves a lot of time, and overall it just results in much more sawing pleasure.

A machine-copied pattern peels off the workpiece cleanly and easily after the sawing operations are completed. Temporary mounting spray adhesives are inexpensive and available from arts, crafts, and photography retail suppliers. Just be sure you get one that states "temporary bond" on the can. It's always a good idea to test your adhesive with scrap paper and a wood sample to be sure the pattern will be easily removed.

If you can, avoid the old method of tracing the pattern from the book and then transferring the traced pattern to the workpiece with carbon paper. If you must do it that way, use *graphite* paper. It is cleaner, less greasy, and the image it leaves is more easily removed with light sanding.

If you decide to use the rubber cement method to bond a machine-copied pattern to the workpiece, a little more care is required. Do not brush on too heavy a coat. If some cement remains on the wood after

Illus. 3   Pressing down a spray-adhesive-coated copy of the pattern directly onto the wood workpiece blank.

peeling off the pattern, it can be removed by rubbing it off with your fingers (**do not use solvents**). Conversely, when temporary bond spray adhesive is properly applied no residue remains on the wood surface. In either case you may want to lightly sand the surfaces very carefully with fine-grit paper (180 grit or smoother) before finishing.

The Basics of Stack-Sawing

Don't forget to use the technique of stack-sawing two or more layers at a time to duplicate parts exactly (Illus. 4). Stacking multiple layers (gang- or plural-sawing) is a good way to increase production by making several cutouts all at once, depending upon individual thickness (Illus. 2). Today ultra-thin plywoods are available to permit stacking many layers. However, you may want to use thin solid woods, as in earlier times, to create historically accurate reproductions of these patterns, since plywood had not been invented then and was not widely used until the 1940s.

Illus. 4 Stapling three layers of plywood together is just one of many ways to hold parts for stack-sawing. Glue, nails, or tape can also be used. When using nails or staples, be sure the points do not protrude through the bottom layer. This would inhibit feeding and scratch the saw table.

The Range of Patterns

We have included patterns for approximately 140 new projects ranging from simple pierced designs to a highly detailed plaque of a steam engine. Nearly 30 categories of pattern types include ornamental numbers and letters, beautiful birds and eagles, signs, wall pockets, silhouettes, a sleigh, wheelbarrows, clocks, frames, shelves, jewelry boxes, fretted candle holders, toy furniture, delicate baskets, crosses, antique cars, and even a moose head.

We would be remiss if we didn't mention three related and helpful books: *Scroll Saw Fretwork Techniques and Projects* (Sterling Publishing Co., New York, 1990), *Scroll Saw Fretwork Patterns* (Sterling Publishing Co., New York, 1989), and *Victorian Scroll Saw Patterns* (Sterling Publishing Co., New York, 1990). *Techniques* offers a study in the historical development of fretwork, as well as the tools, techniques, materials, and project styles that have evolved over the past 130 years. The book also covers some modern scroll-sawing machines, and state-of-the-art fretwork along with fine-scroll-sawing techniques. Those books in combination with the detailed classic patterns presented here make this fascinating class of woodworking more fun and at the same time faster and a whole lot easier than it ever was before.

Patterns

Fancy Birds

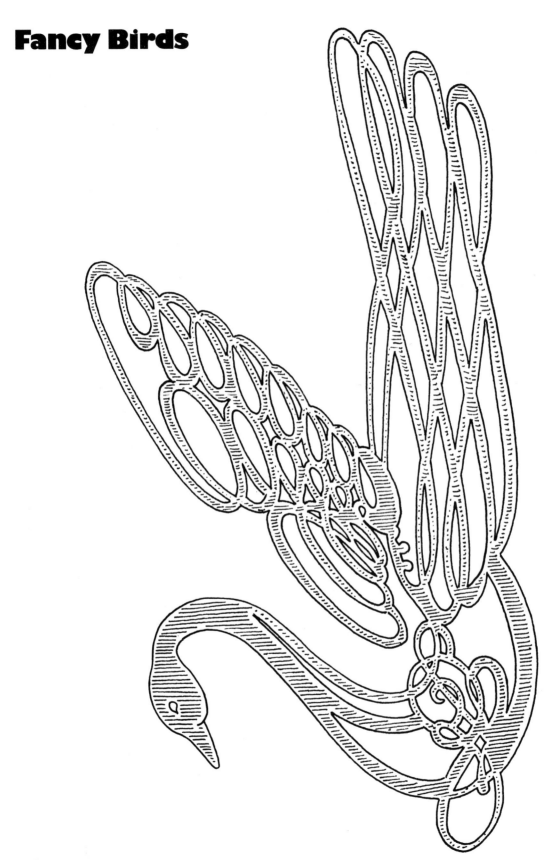

A

B

16

Silhouettes

19

21

27

29

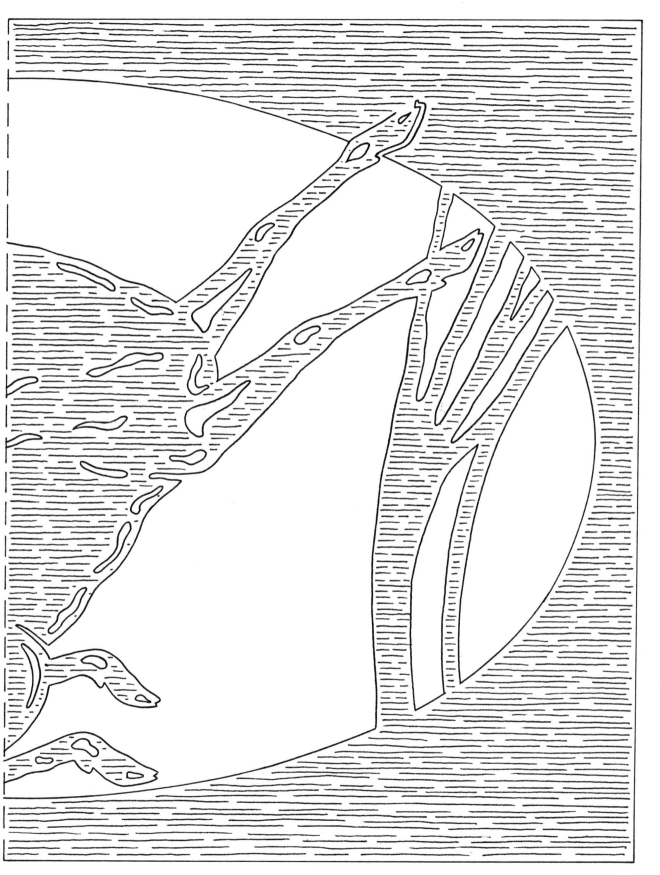

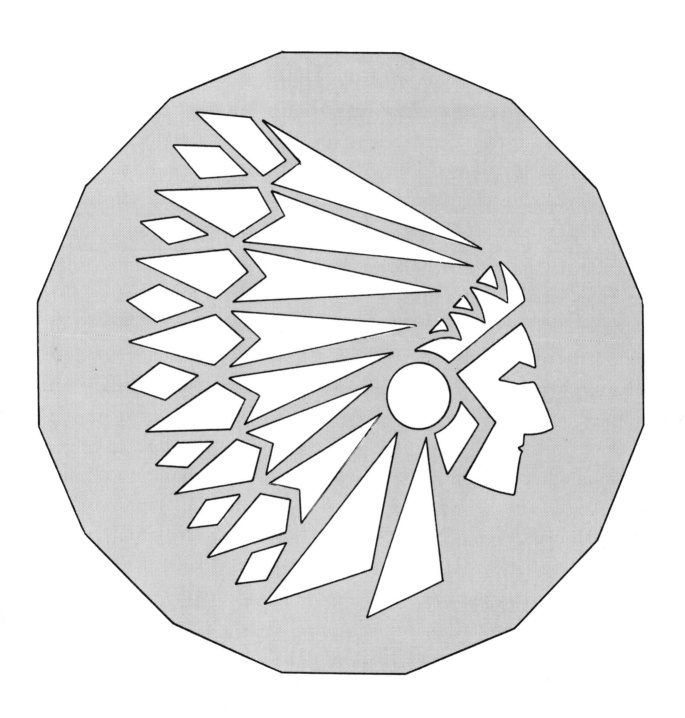

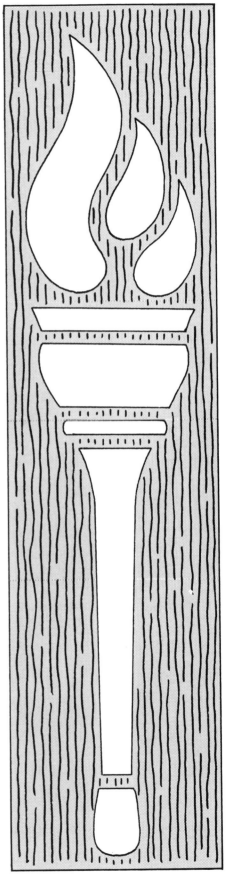

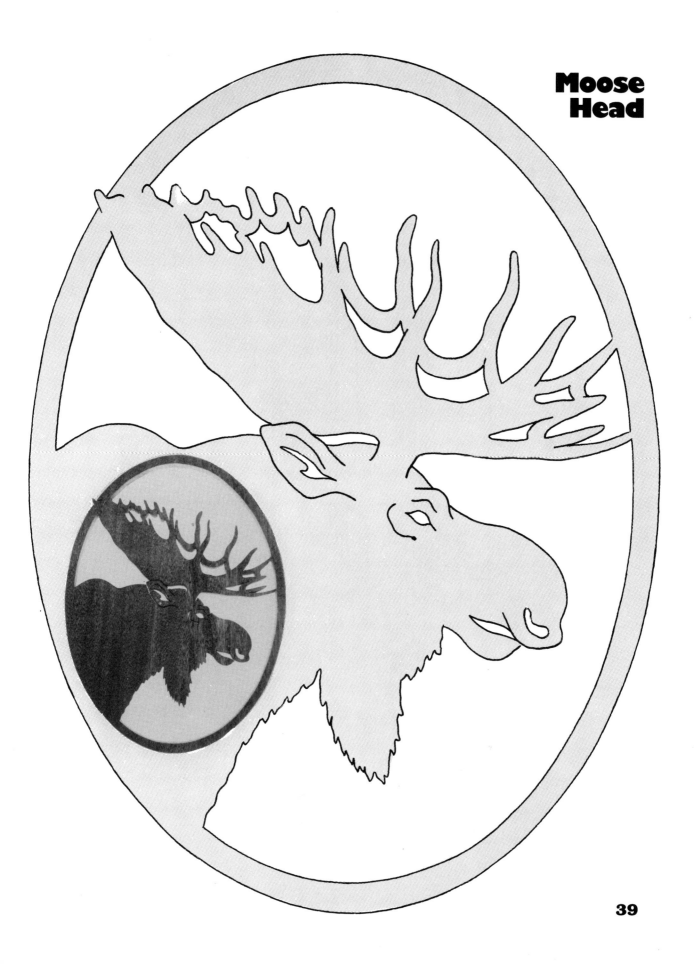

Stars and Stripes

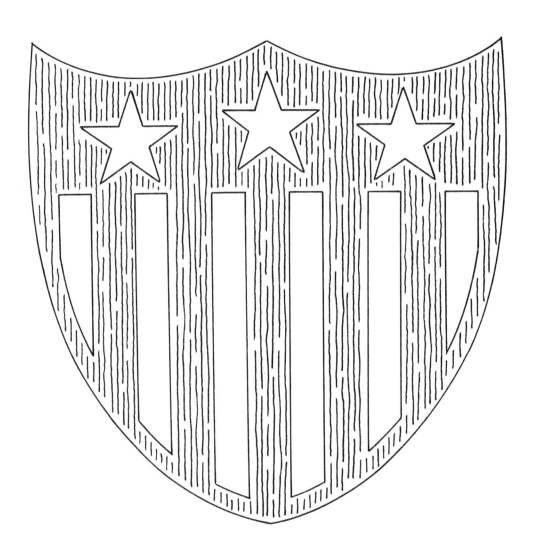

Clock Shelf

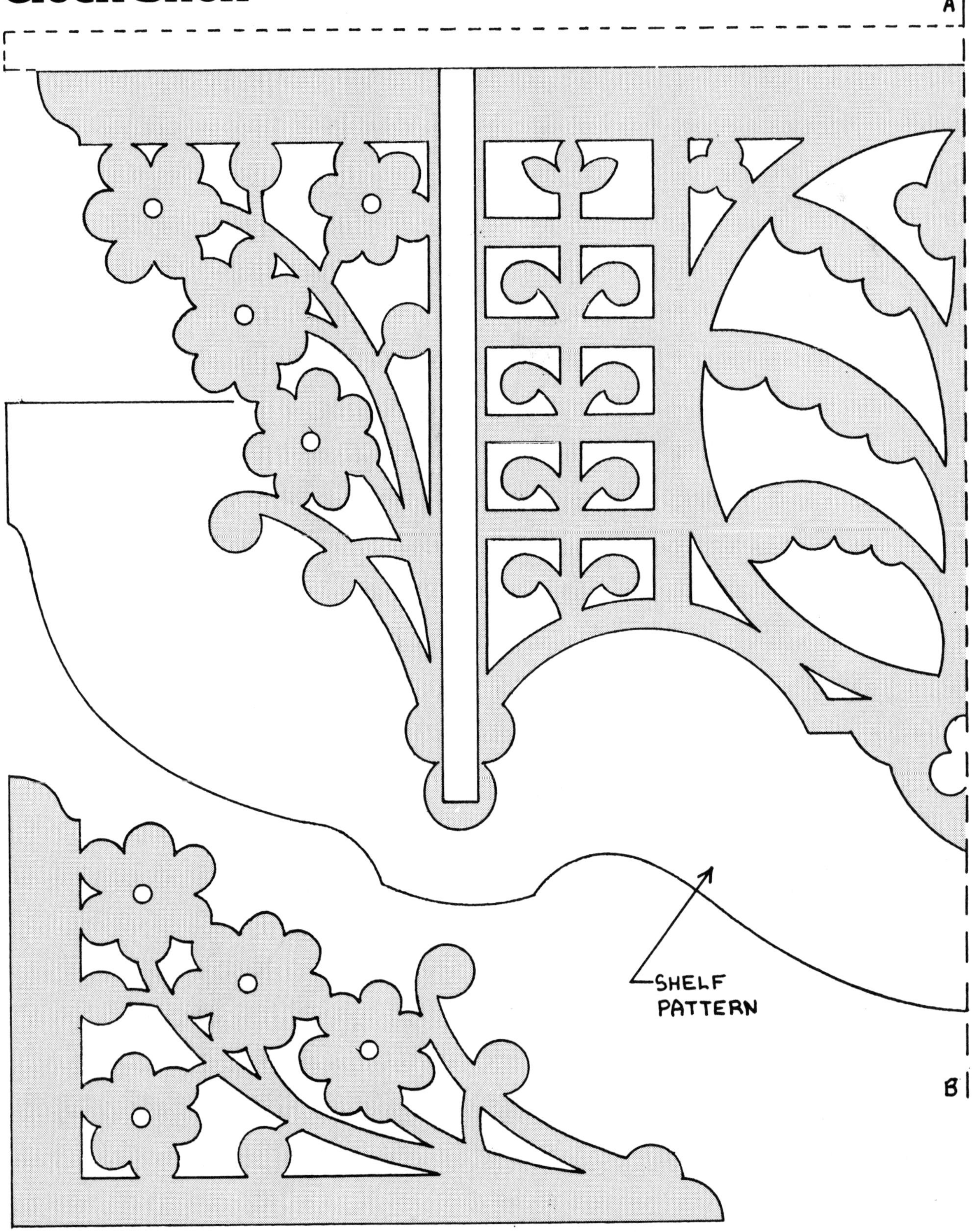

A

B

SHELF
PATTERN

A

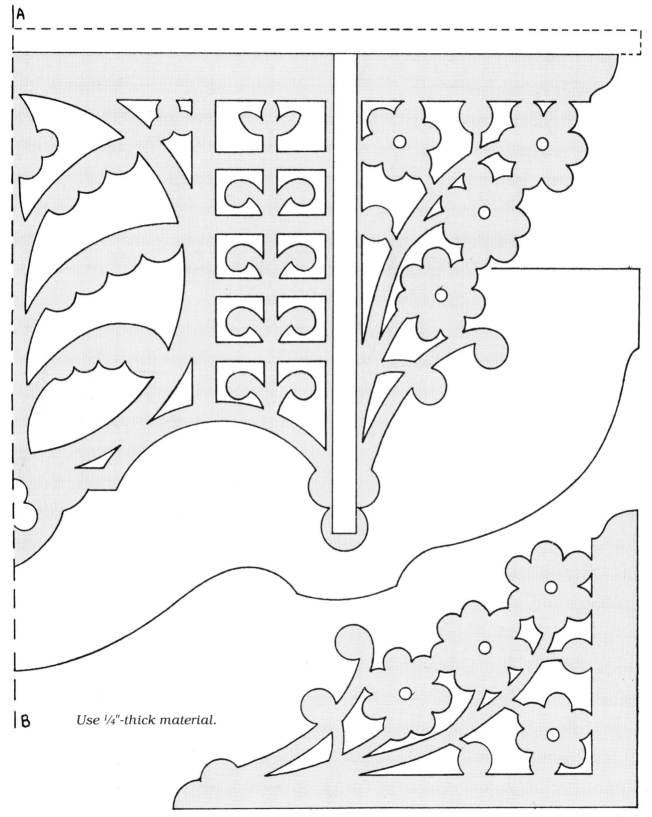

B *Use ¼″-thick material.*

43

Fancy Numbers

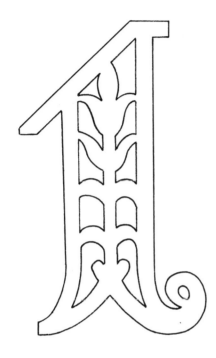

Fancy Alphabet

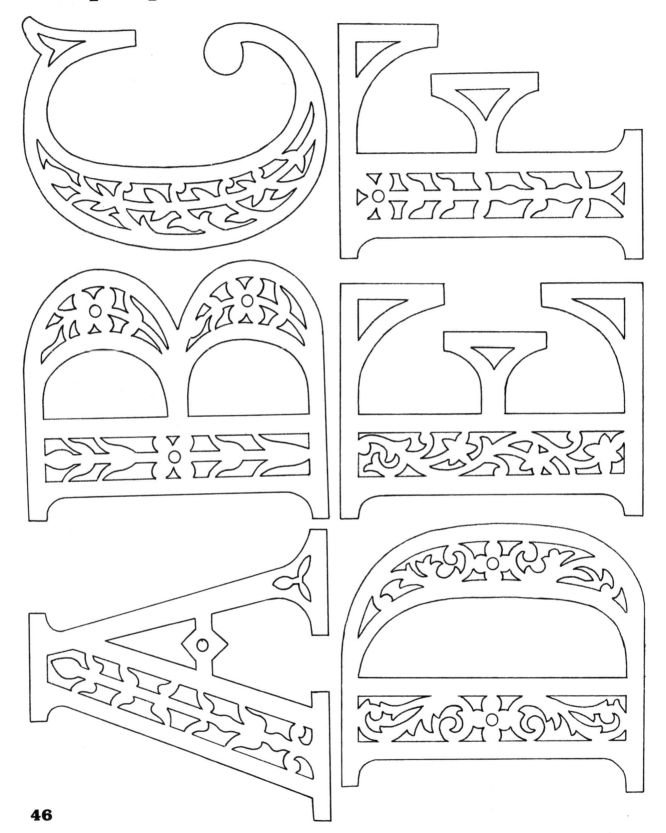

48

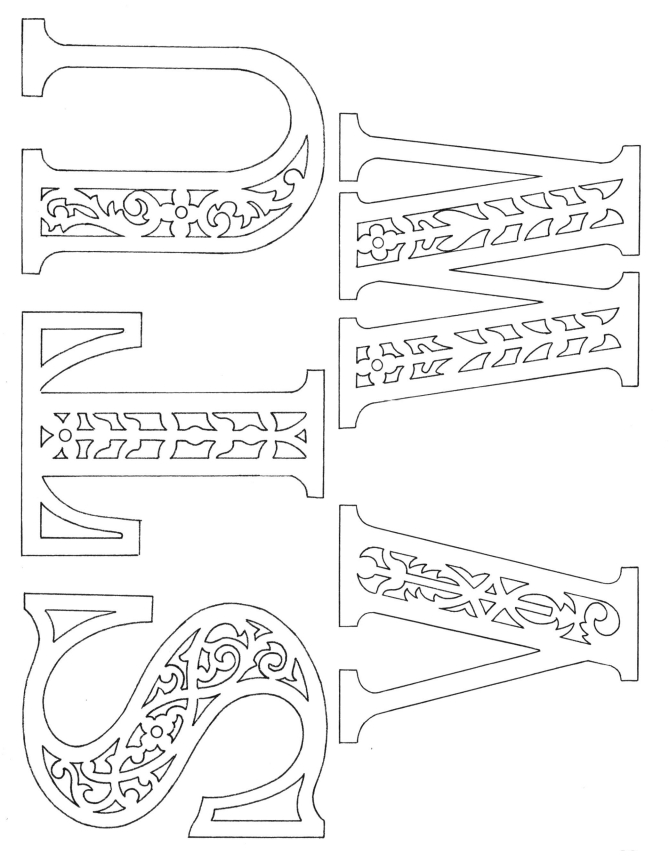

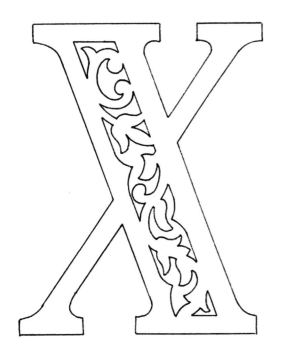
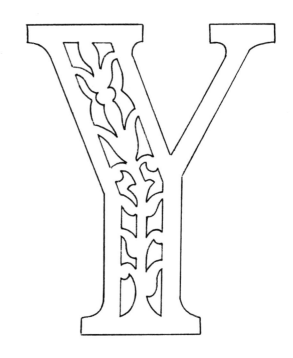
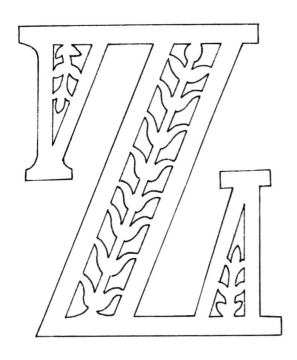

Match Box

SANDPAPER

MATCHES

Welcome Sign

A

B

52

A

B

53

Wall Pockets

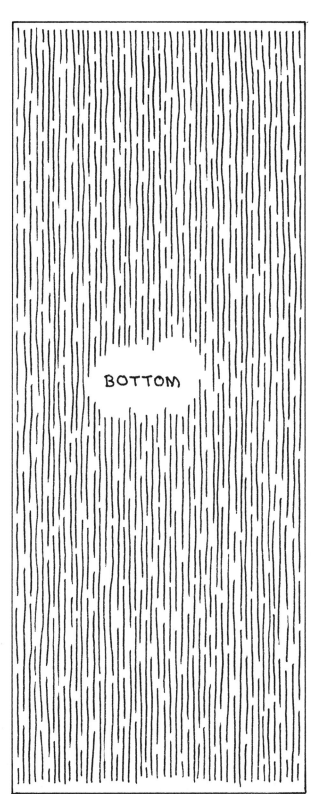

BOTTOM

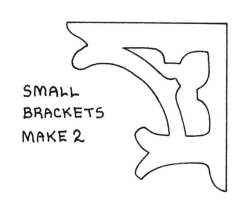

SMALL
BRACKETS
MAKE 2

MIDDLE
BRACKET

ENDS-MAKE 2

57

Wall pocket.
Use ¼″ material and cut bottom to fit.

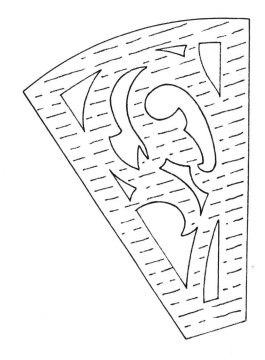

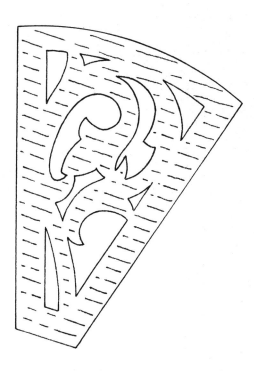

Wall pocket.
Use ⅛″—¼″ material.

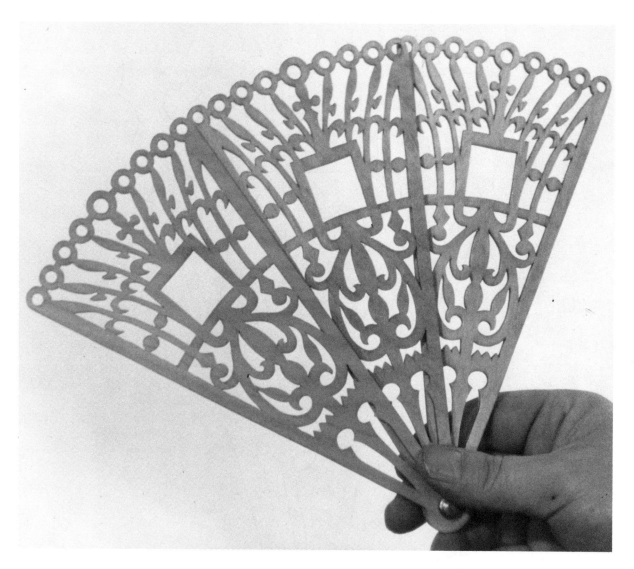

Fan made of three stack-sawn pieces of ⅛″ or 3 mm baltic birch plywood. Assemble at bottom pivots with a brass paper fastener. (See Illus. 1–4 in the introduction.)

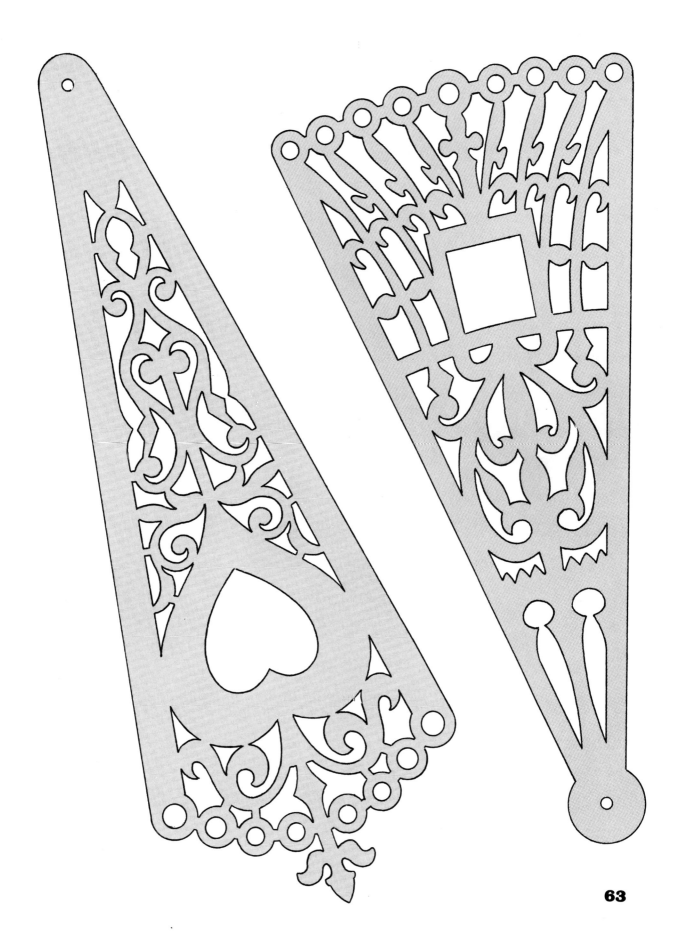

Sleigh

Sleigh. Make from ¼"-thick material.

FRONT
PANEL

SIDE VIEW

UPPER
REAR
PANEL

SIDE VIEW

LOWER
REAR
PANEL

65

MAKE BOTTOM PANEL
5"W x 5⅛"L . BEVEL
END TO FIT AS SHOWN.

A

B

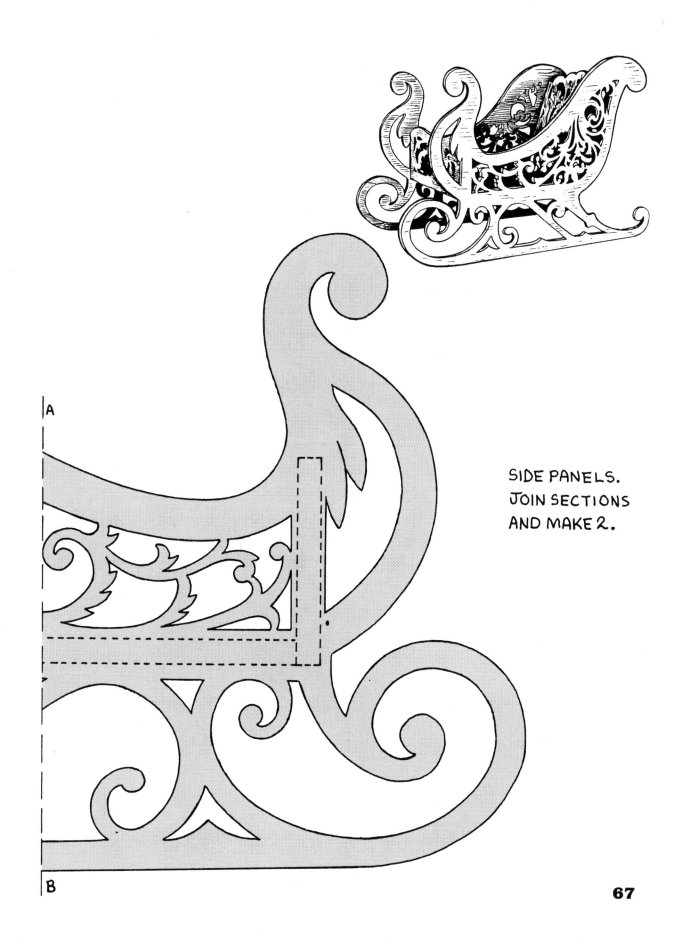

A

B

SIDE PANELS.
JOIN SECTIONS
AND MAKE 2.

67

Jewelry Boxes

Jewelry box design no. 1. Make from ³⁄₈"-thick material through-out for this box, but use ¹⁄₈" or less for the overlay design on the lid.

Typical details shown on this box include mitred corners, use of a ³⁄₄"-wide by 5" continuous hinge, and the use of a colored cardboard backer lining the inside of the front and ends.

TOP — $\frac{3}{8}''$ THICK

OVERLAY — USE $\frac{1}{8}''$ THICK MATERIAL OF CONTRASTING COLOR

FRONT PANEL

MAKE REAR PANEL SAME SIZE WITHOUT INTERIOR CUTOUTS

SIDE PANELS – MAKE 2

70

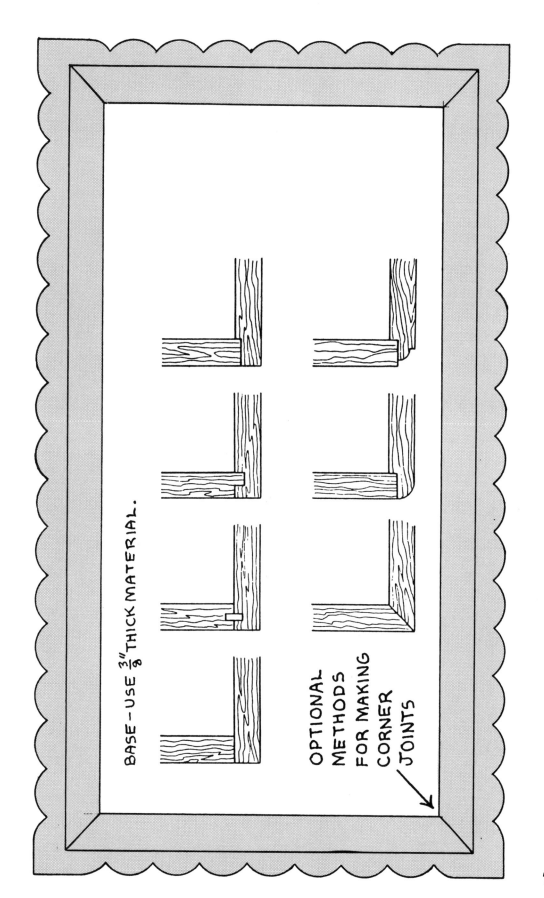

BASE—USE $\frac{3}{8}$" THICK MATERIAL.

OPTIONAL
METHODS
FOR MAKING
CORNER JOINTS

71

Jewelry box design no. 2. The lid design can be pierced or in-laid in a contrasting wood.

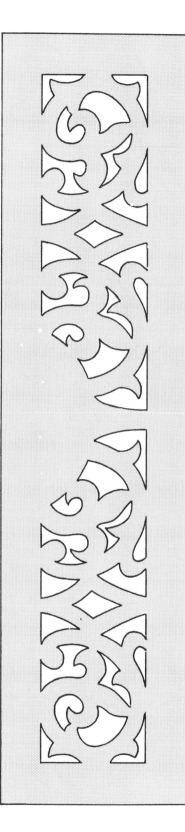

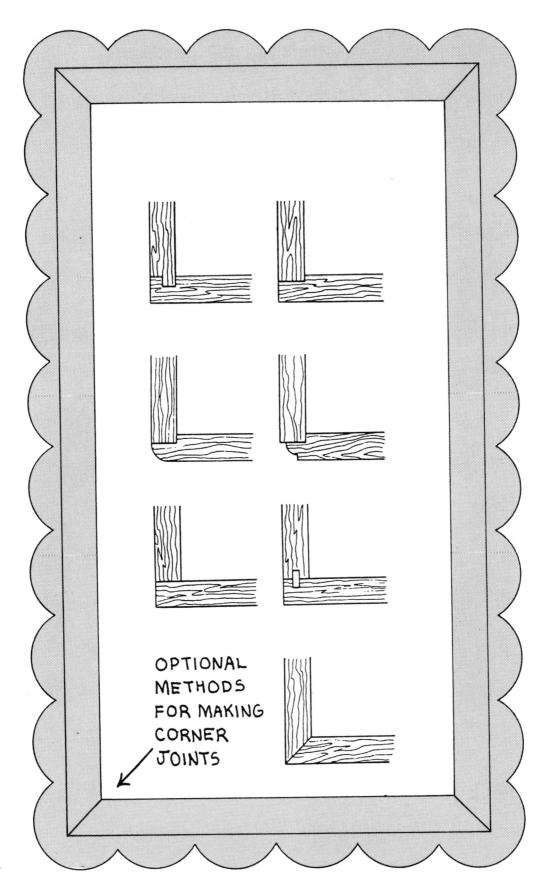

OPTIONAL
METHODS
FOR MAKING
CORNER
JOINTS

This toy cradle is made from 3/16"-thick wood. Notice the through-mortise and tab joints that connect the sides and bottom to the ends.

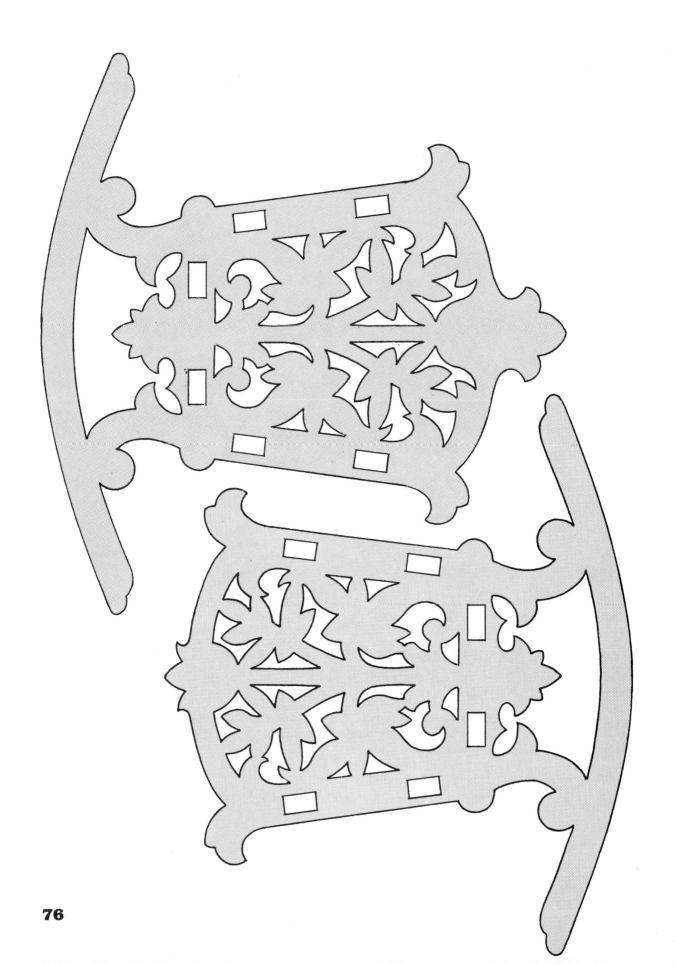

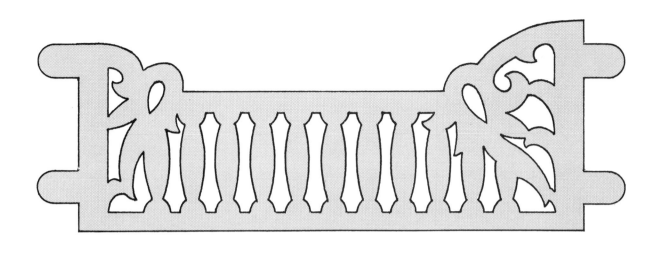

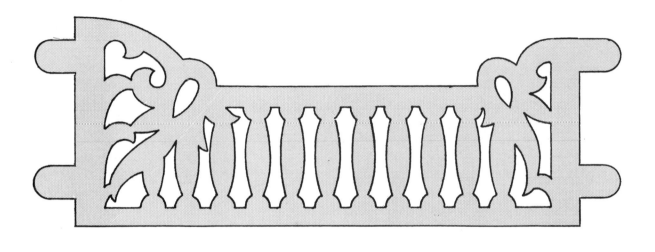

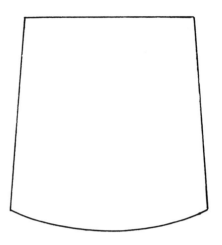

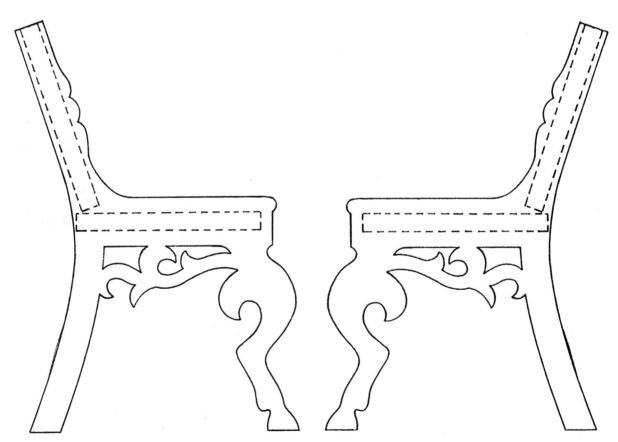

BEVEL OUTERMOST EDGES
(SLIGHTLY) TO MATCH
ANGLE OF SIDE PIECES
PRODUCED BY SEAT

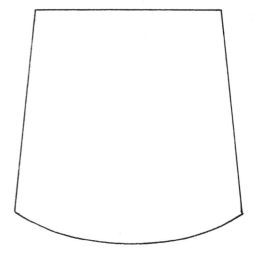

SEAT CAN BE COVERED
WITH COLORED FABRIC.

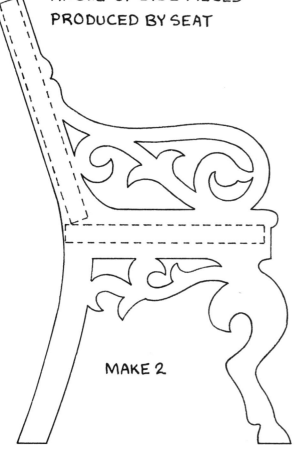

MAKE 2

BEVEL
OUTERMOST
EDGES OF
BACKPIECE
(SLIGHTLY)
TO FIT.

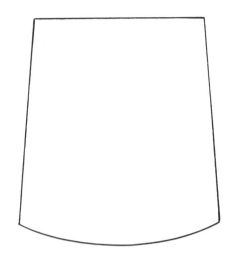

USE $\frac{3}{16}$" THICK MATERIAL.
SEAT CAN BE COVERED
WITH COLORED FABRIC.

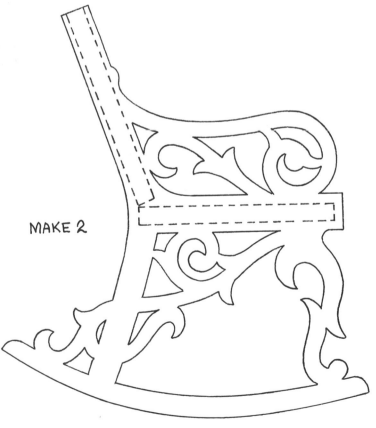

MAKE 2

MAKE 2

Table with through-mortise and tab construction. Use ³⁄₁₆″-thick material. Cut two legs and two apron pieces.

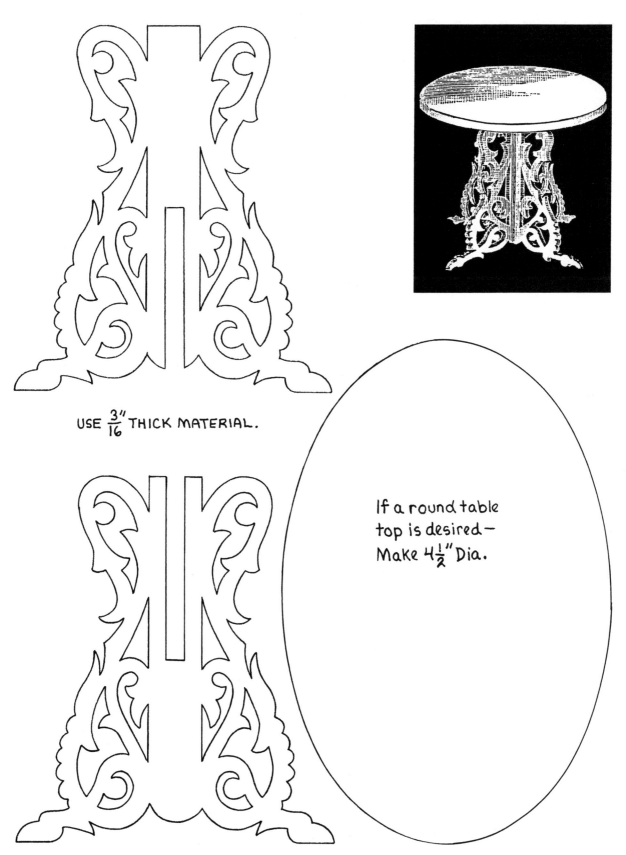

USE $\frac{3''}{16}$ THICK MATERIAL.

If a round table
top is desired —
Make $4\frac{1}{2}''$ Dia.

Toy bed. Use ³⁄₁₆"-thick material and cut a bottom to fit.

Easels

Easel, one of several designs. Make all easels from ¼"-thick material. Supporting legs or struts can be hinged in several ways. (See the methods of hinging below.)

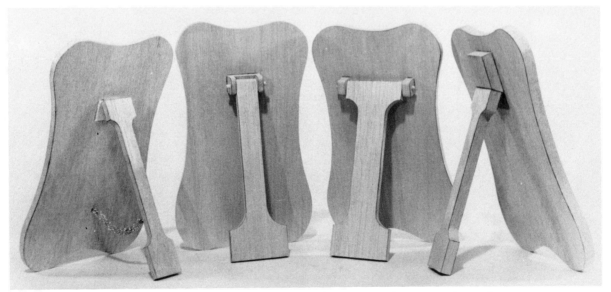

Some ways of hinging supporting legs or struts on easels and backers of photo/mirror frames. Left: a fabric or leather hinge with a chain retainer; middle: two types of dowel pivots; and right: a small metal hinge with a bevelled stop block.

Small easel. Use ⅛″-thick material. Make ledge ½″ wide by 3½″ long. (See the methods of hinging opposite.)

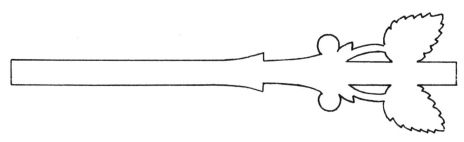

Easel. Cut from ¼″-thick material. Make ledge ¾″ wide by 5¼″ long. (See the methods of hinging on page 86.)

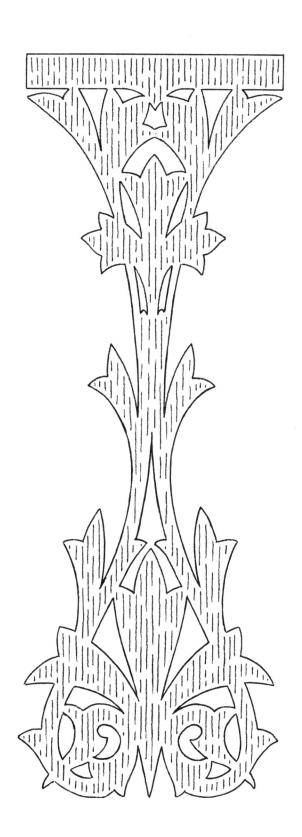

90

Easel. Use ¼"-thick material. Cut ledge 34" wide by 5½" long. (See the methods of hinging on page 86.)

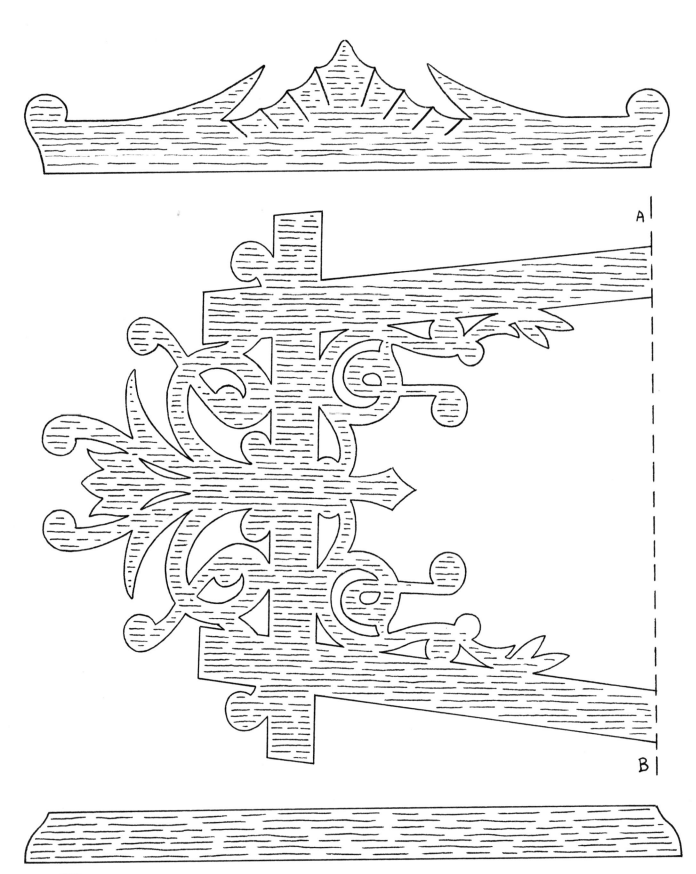

A

B

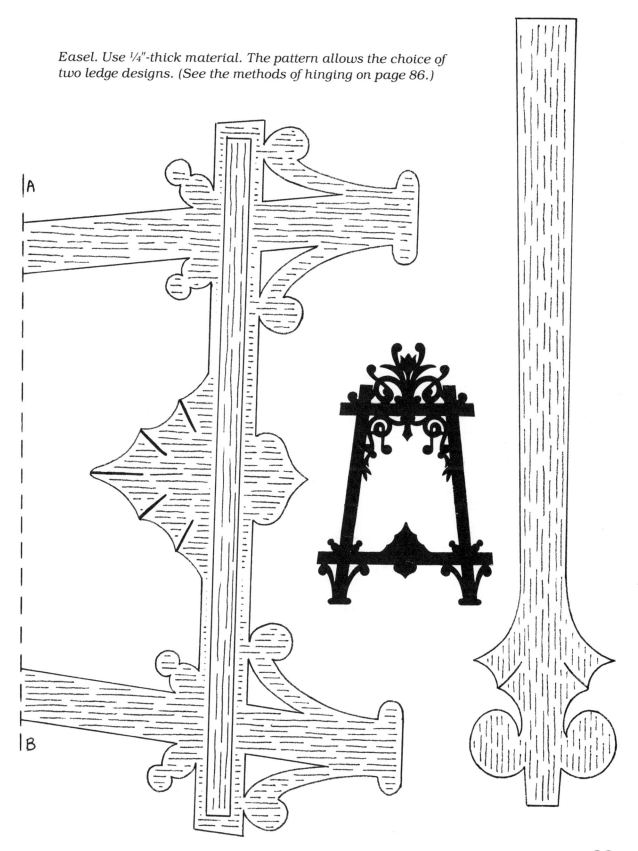

Easel. Use ¼″-thick material. The pattern allows the choice of two ledge designs. (See the methods of hinging on page 86.)

A

B

93

Picture/Mirror Frames

OVERLAY

B

A

100

Victorian frame with overlay.

B

A

Standing frame. Cut two leg pieces.

108

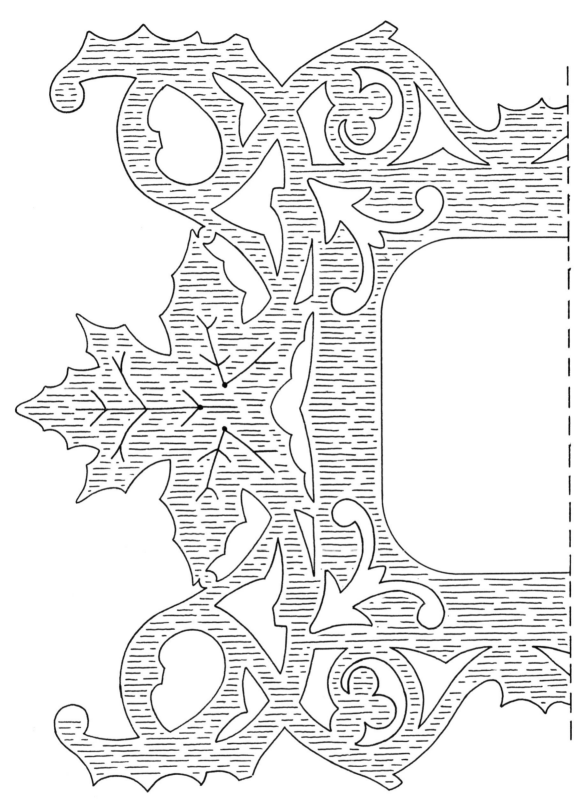

Make the four corner overlay decorations of thin, contrasting material.

111

B

A

B

A

115

Bird mantle clock. Order movement with shaft length suitable to wood material thickness used and the required 2¾"-diameter clock dial from Reidle Products, Box 661, Richland Center, WI 53581.

Two of four mini-clock designs. Movements are 1⅜"-diameter. Mini-clock inserts available from the Klockit Co., Box 636, Lake Geneva, WI 53147.

BORE EXACTLY
$1\frac{3}{8}$" DIA. HOLES
FOR CLOCK
MOVEMENTS.

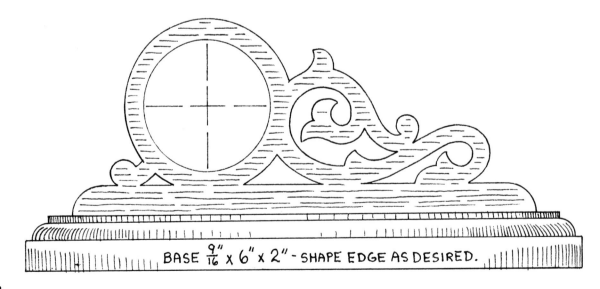

BASE $\frac{9}{16}$" x 6" x 2" - SHAPE EDGE AS DESIRED.

BORE EXACTLY
$1\frac{3}{8}''$ DIA. HOLES
FOR CLOCK
MOVEMENTS.

Cut upright piece from ¼"- to ½"-thick material. Order movement with appropriate shaft length. (See the drawings on pages 118 and 119.) Make the base ¾" by 2½" by 11½".

Bavarian clock, similar to the pattern that follows.

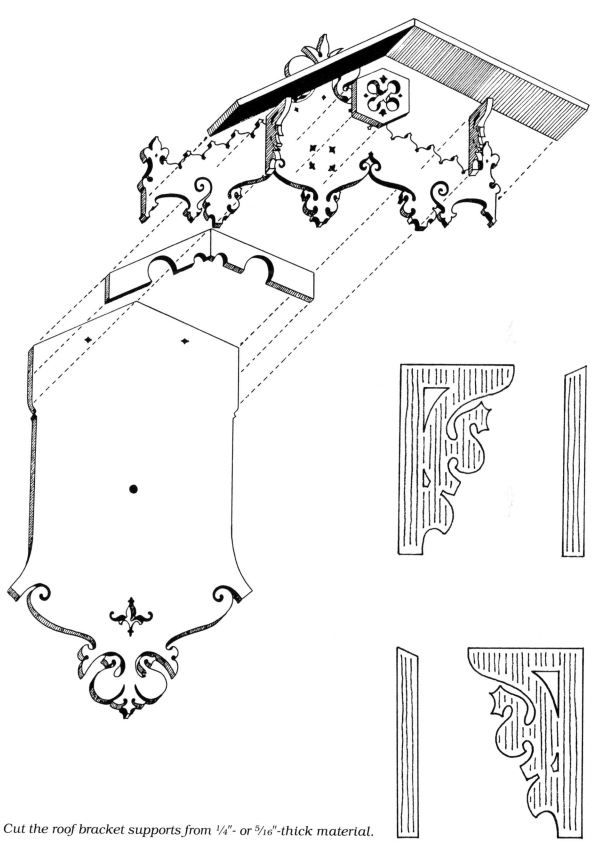

Cut the roof bracket supports from ¹⁄₄″- or ⁵⁄₁₆″-thick material.

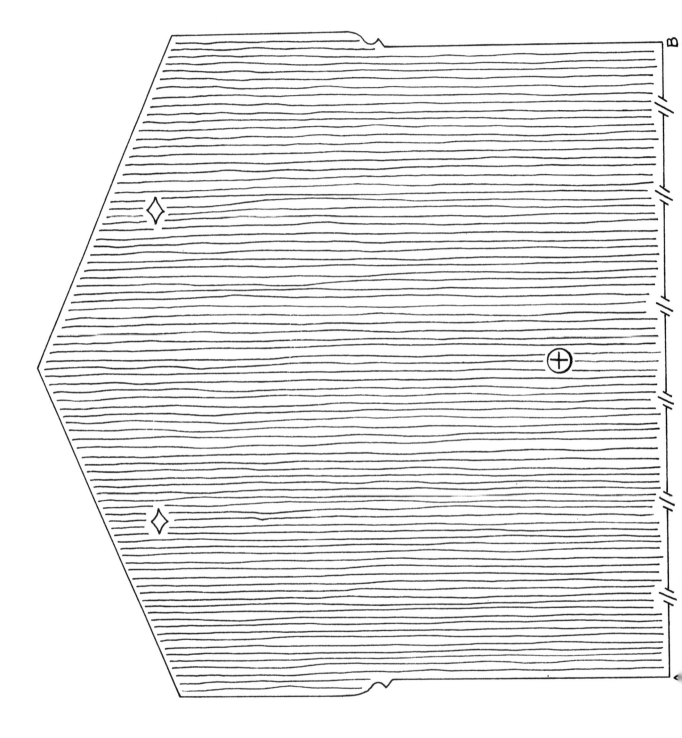

B

Cut from ¼"- to ⅜"-thick material.

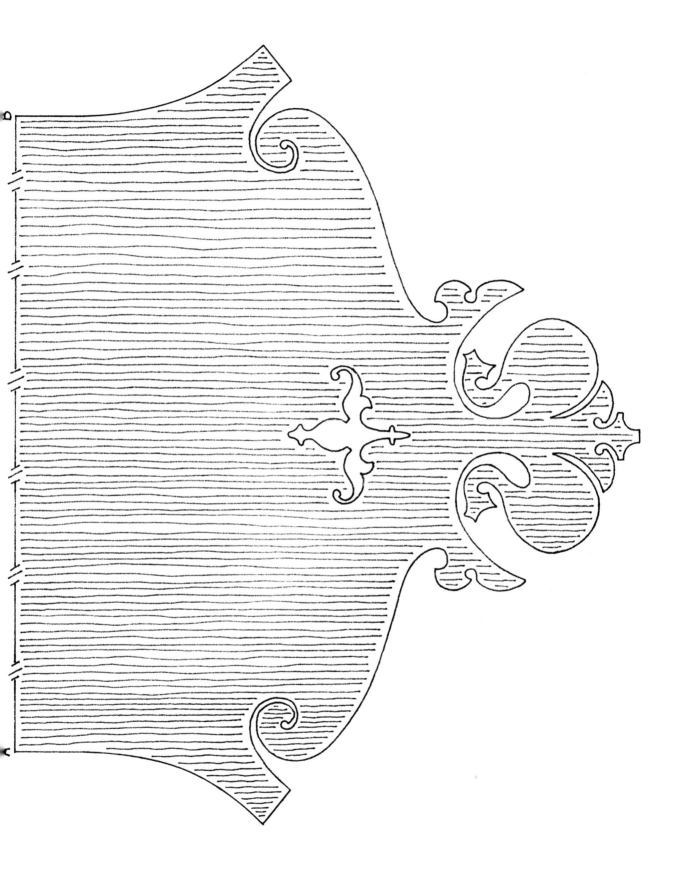

Cut from ¼″- to ⅜″-thick material.

A

B

127

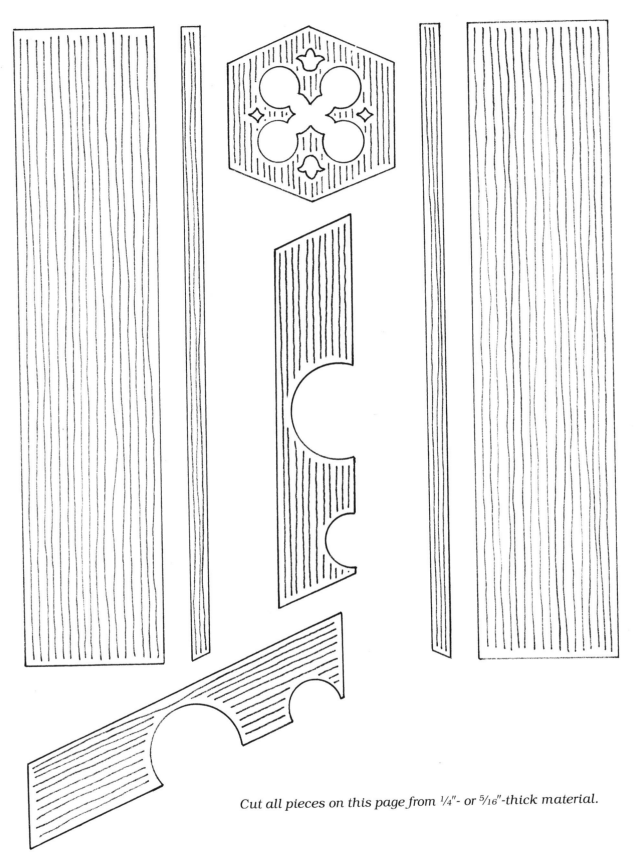

Cut all pieces on this page from ¹/₄″- or ⁵/₁₆″-thick material.

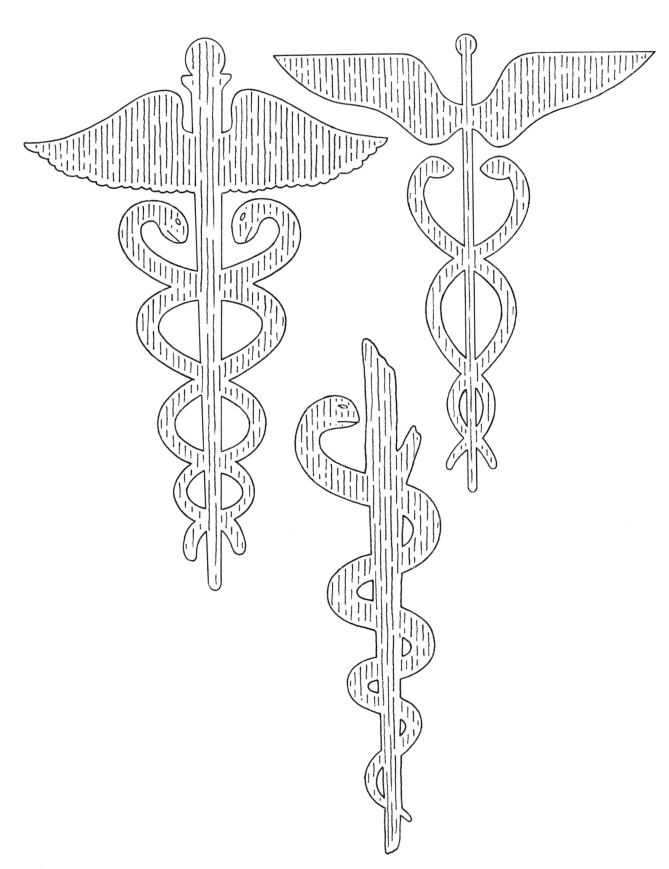

Antique Cars

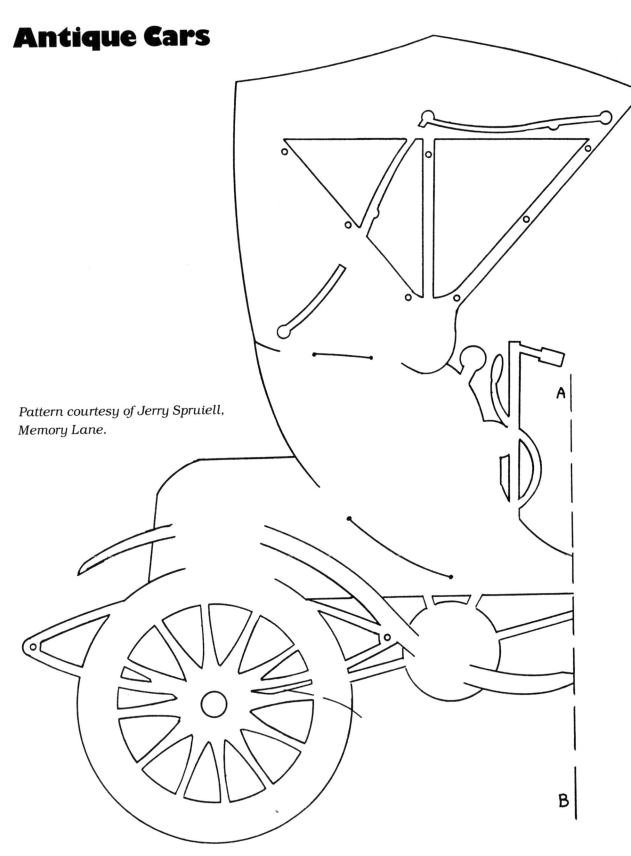

Pattern courtesy of Jerry Spruiell,
Memory Lane.

A

B

1903 STUDEBAKER

A

B

Pattern courtesy of Jerry Spruiell, Memory Lane.

A

B

A

1914 CHEVROLET ROADSTER

B

135

Steam Engine

A

B

A

B

Baskets

Basket with slanted sides. Make from ¼"-thick material, and cut bottom to fit.

MITRE CORNERS
MAKE BOTTOM TO FIT

Basket. Use ¼″-thick material.

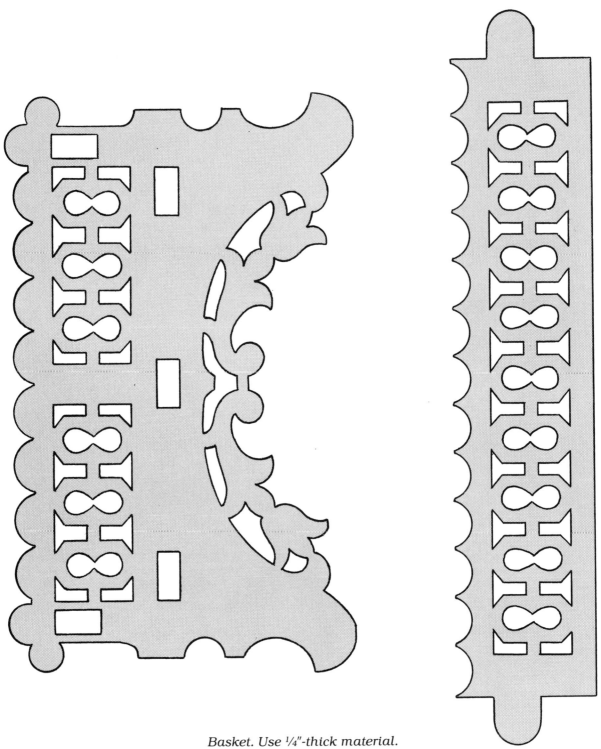

Basket. Use ¼″-thick material.

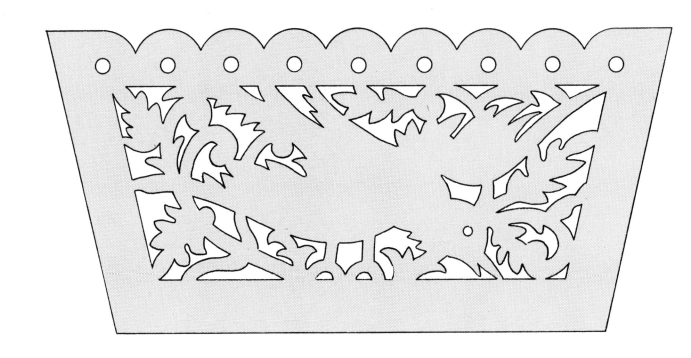

SIDE PANELS- MAKE 2 EACH – MITRE CORNERS

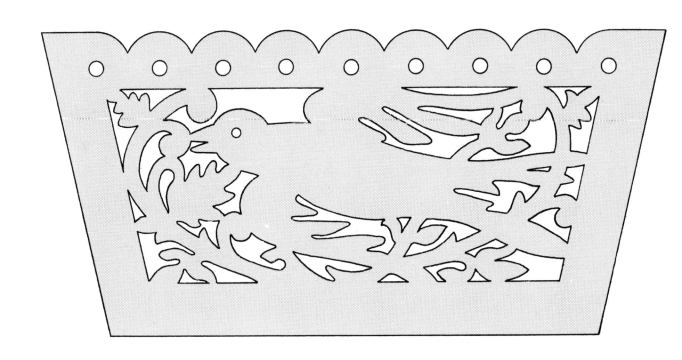

Basket. Use ¼"-thick material.

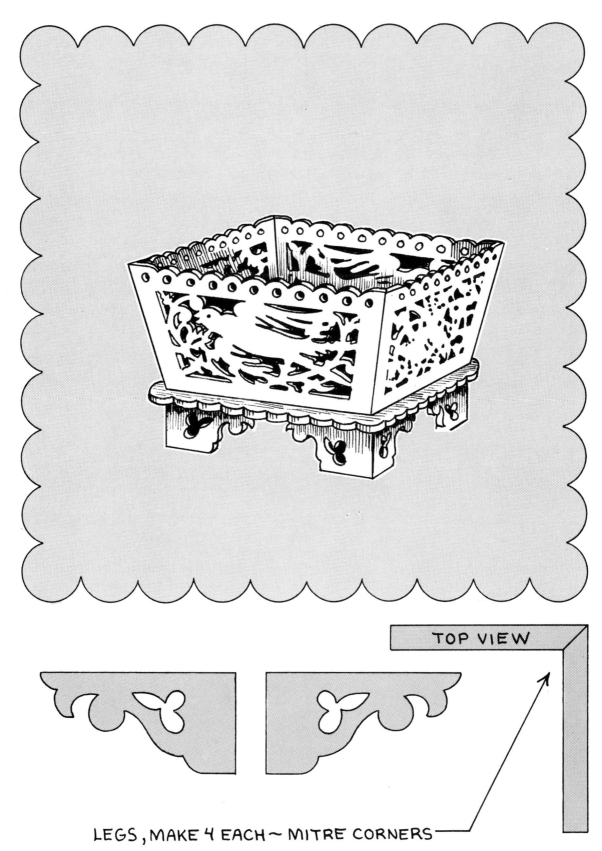

LEGS, MAKE 4 EACH ~ MITRE CORNERS

TOP VIEW

This beautiful lidded basket is made from $^5/_{16}''$-thick solid oak.

The lids are hinged with dowel pivots.

A close-up look at the hinge dowels and the through-mortise and tab construction details.

Notice the edge of each lid is rounded over for clearance.

145

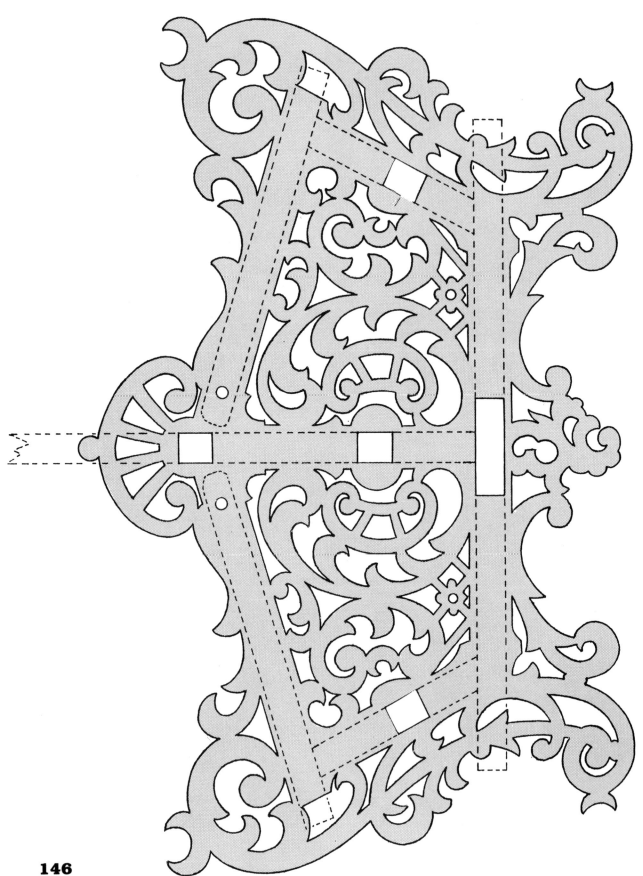

UP ↑

148

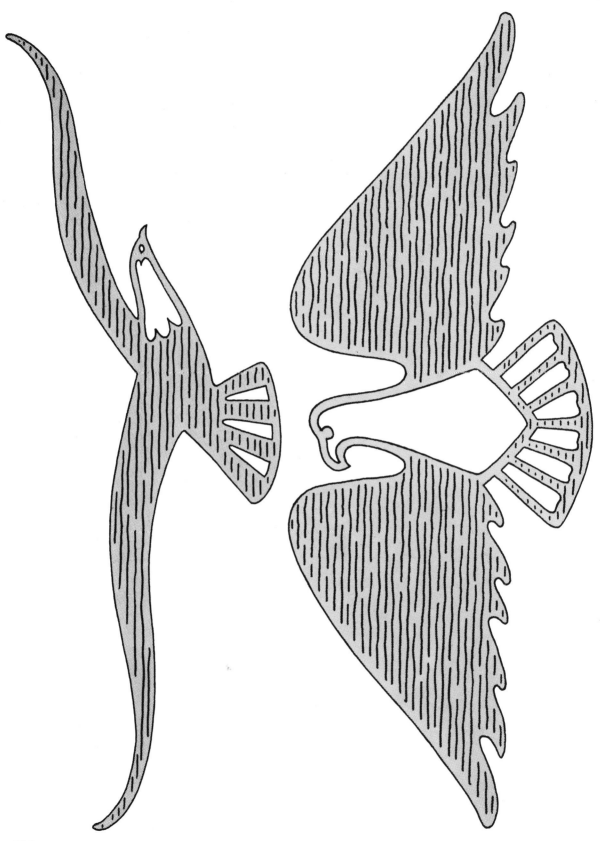

Wall thermometer. Use glue on thermometer card, 3″ long, available from Constantine & Sons, 2050 Eastchester Rd., Bronx, NY 10461.

152

Candelabrum and candle holder set.

Cut two identical pieces with matching halved slot cuts, sawing one on the solid line and the other on the dashed line.

Cut two identical pieces with matching halved slot cuts, sawing one on the solid line and the other on the dashed line.

155

Candle holder set made from ¼″-thick material. Note: When using plywood, be advised that actual thickness may vary from ¼″ to slightly less.

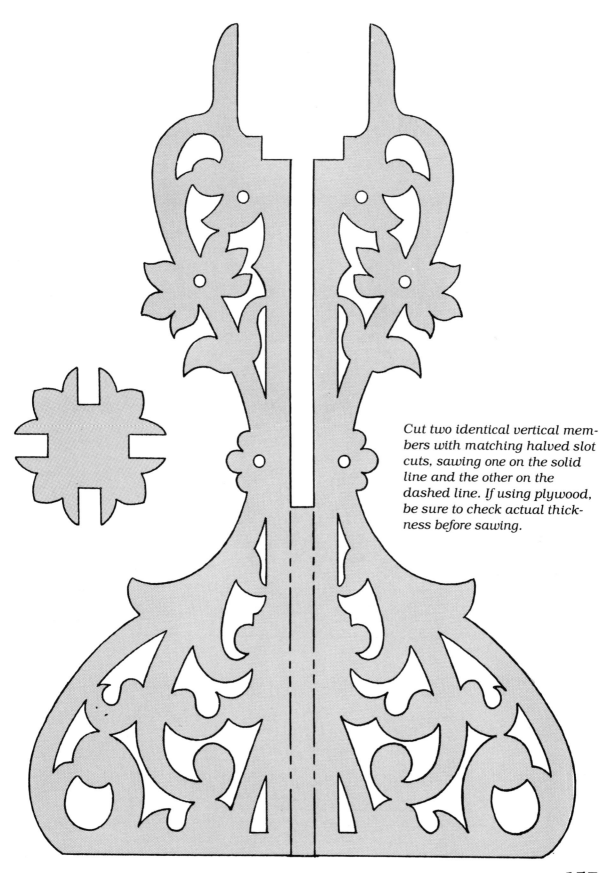

Cut two identical vertical members with matching halved slot cuts, sawing one on the solid line and the other on the dashed line. If using plywood, be sure to check actual thickness before sawing.

Cut two identical vertical members with matching halved slot cuts, sawing one on the solid line and the other on the dashed line. If using plywood, be sure to check actual thickness before sawing.

Corner shelf made of ¼"-thick material.

A

B

162

Deer shelf. Note optional deer head pattern design for more strength.

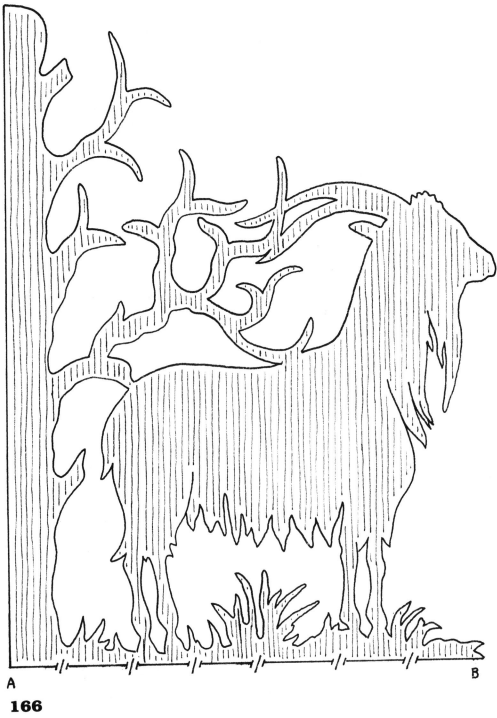

A

B

166

A   B

A   B

A B

171

Ships

Wheelbarrows

FRONT PANEL

FRONT PANEL OVERLAY

SIDES — MAKE 2

WHEELS — MAKE 2

MAKE 2

MAKE A BOTTOM TO FIT. $3\frac{1}{2}$" WIDE.

Wheelbarrow. Cut from 3/16"- or 1/4"-thick material. Use 1/4"-diameter dowel cut to the appropriate length for axle.

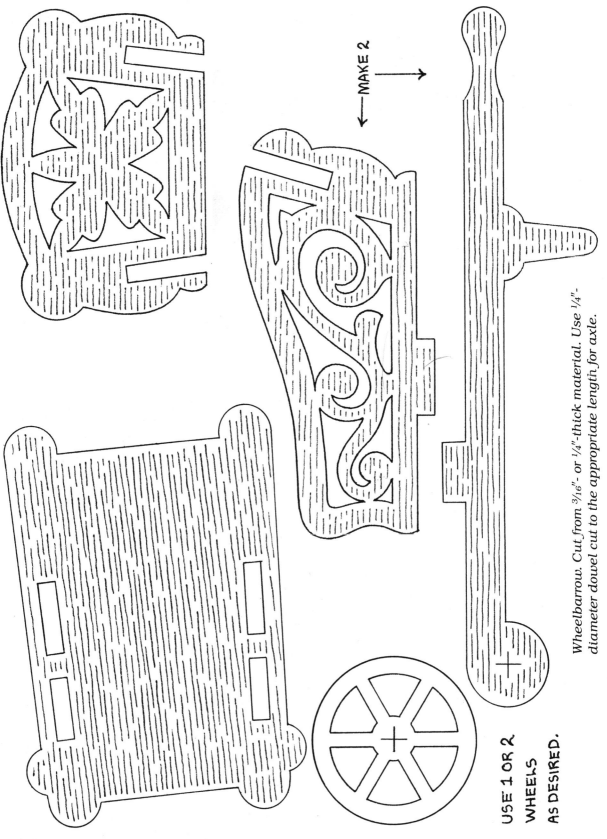

MAKE 2 →

USE 1 OR 2
WHEELS
AS DESIRED.

Wheelbarrow. Cut from 3/16"- or 1/4"-thick material. Use 1/4"-diameter dowel cut to the appropriate length for axle.

A

B

176

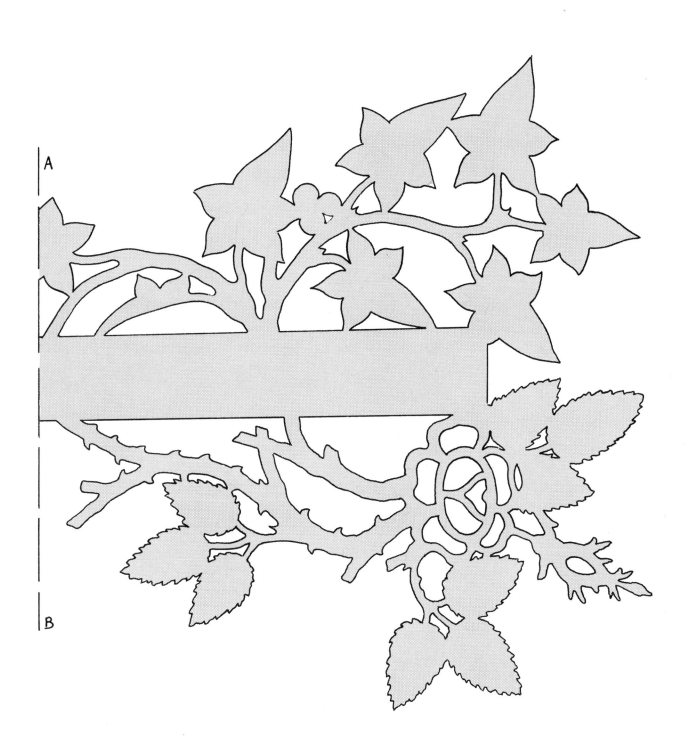

A

B

177

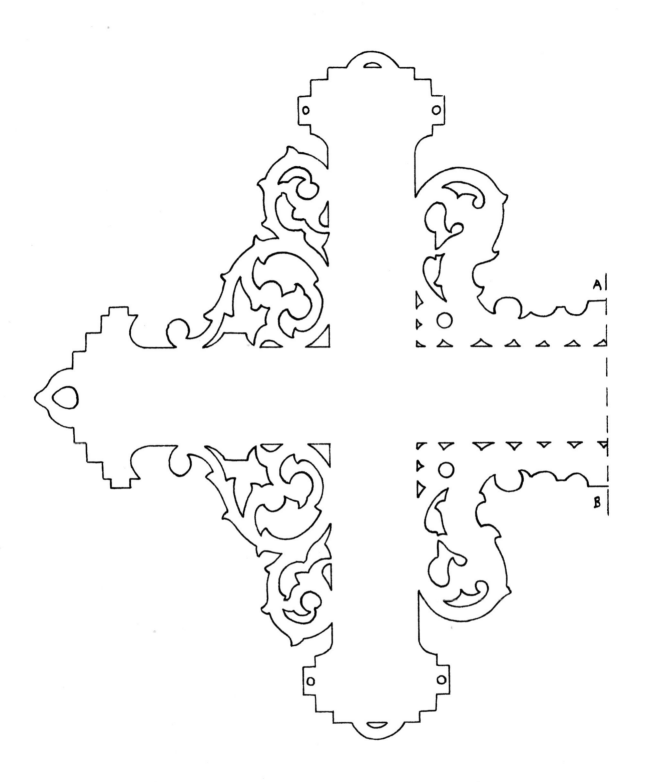

A

B

179

Thimble Holder

ROOF PANELS

181

Miscellaneous Designs

A

B

183

About the Authors

Patrick Spielman's love of wood began when, as a child, he transformed fruit crates into toys. Now this prolific and innovative woodworker is respected worldwide as a teacher and author.

His most famous contribution to the woodworking field has been his perfection of a method to season green wood with polyethylene glycol 1000 (PEG). He went on to invent, manufacture, and distribute the PEG-Thermovat chemical seasoning system.

During his many years as shop instructor in Wisconsin, Spielman published manuals, teaching guides, and more than 24 popular books, including *Modern Wood Technology*, a college text. He also wrote six educational series on wood technology, tool use, processing techniques, design, and wood-product planning.

Author of the best-selling *Router Handbook*, Spielman has served as editorial consultant to a professional magazine and as advisor and consultant to power tool manufacturers, and his products, techniques, and many books have been featured in numerous periodicals.

This pioneer of new ideas and inventor of countless jigs, fixtures, and designs used throughout the world is a unique combination of expert woodworker and brilliant teacher—all of which have endeared him to his many readers and to his publisher.

At Spielmans Wood Works in the woods of northern Door County, Wisconsin, he and his family create and sell some of the most durable and popular furniture products and designs available.

Coauthor James Reidle has been doing fancy woodwork along with general carpentry work all his life. He grew up watching his father create magnificent pieces of scroll-saw fretwork on treadle-type scroll saws. Years later, he wanted to recapture the best features of the early scroll saws his father used, so he developed one of his own, which is especially designed for fretwork and fine-detail scroll sawing. In addition, Reidle developed the first mail-order business in a number of years that is mainly devoted to fretwork patterns and supplies.

Should you wish to contact Patrick Spielman or James Reidle, please send your letters to Sterling Publishing Company.

Current Books by Patrick Spielman

Alphabets and Designs for Wood Signs.
50 alphabet patterns, plans for many decorative designs, the latest on hand carving, routing, cutouts, and sandblasting. Pricing data. Photo gallery (4 pages in color) of wood signs by professionals from across the U.S. Over 200 illustrations. 128 pages.

Carving Large Birds. Spielman and renowned woodcarver Bill Dehos show how to carve a fascinating array of large birds. All of the tools and basic techniques that are used are discussed in depth, and hundreds of photos, illustrations, and patterns are provided for carving graceful swans, majestic eagles, comical-looking penguins, a variety of owls, and scores of other birds. Oversized. 16 pages in full color. 192 pages.

Carving Wild Animals: Life-Size Wood Figures. Spielman and renowned woodcarver Bill Dehos show how to carve more than 20 magnificent creatures of the North American wild. A cougar, black bear, prairie dog, squirrel, raccoon, and fox are some of the life-size animals included. Step-by-step, photo-filled instructions and multiple view

patterns, plus tips on the use of tools, wood selection, finishing, and polishing help you bring each animal to life. Oversized. Over 300 photos; 16 pages in full color. 240 pages.

Gluing & Clamping. A thorough, up-to-date examination of one of the most critical steps in woodworking. Spielman explores the features of every type of glue—from traditional animal-hide glues to the newest epoxies—the clamps and tools needed, the bonding properties of different wood species, safety tips, and all techniques from edge-to-edge and end-to-end gluing to applying plastic laminates. Also included is a glossary of terms. Over 500 illustrations. 256 pages.

Making Country-Rustic Wood Projects.
Hundreds of photos, patterns, and detailed scaled drawings reveal construction methods, woodworking techniques, and Spielman's professional secrets for making indoor and outdoor furniture in the distinctly attractive Country-Rustic style. Covered are all aspects of furniture making

from choosing the best wood for the job to texturing smooth boards. Among the dozens of projects are mailboxes, cabinets, shelves, coffee tables, weather vanes, doors, panelling, plant stands and many other durable and economical pieces. 400 illustrations. 4 pages in full color. 164 pages.

Making Wood Decoys. A clear step-by-step approach to the basics of decoy carving. This book is abundantly illustrated with closeup photos for designing, selecting, and obtaining woods; tools; feather detailing; painting; and finishing of decorative and working decoys. Six different professional decoy artists are featured. Photo gallery (4 pages in full color) along with numerous detailed plans for various popular decoys. 160 pages.

Making Wood Signs. Designing, selecting woods and tools, and every process through finishing are clearly covered. Hand-carved, power-carved, routed, and sandblasted processes in small to huge signs are presented. Foolproof guides for professional letters and ornaments. Hundreds of photos (4 pages in full color). Lists sources for supplies and special tooling. 144 pages.

Realistic Decoys. Spielman and master carver Keith Bridenhagen reveal their successful techniques for carving, feather-texturing, painting, and finishing wood decoys. Details that you can't find elsewhere—anatomy, attitudes, markings, and the easy step-by-step approach to perfect delicate procedures—make this book invaluable. Includes listings for contests, shows, and sources of tools and supplies. 274 closeup photos. 28 in color. 224 pages.

Router Basics. With over 200 closeup step-by-step photos and drawings, this valuable overview will guide the new owner as well as provide a spark to owners for whom the router isn't the tool they turn to most often. Covers all the basic router styles, along with how-it-works descrip-

tions of all its major features. Includes sections on bits and accessories as well as square-cutting and trimming, case and furniture routing, cutting circles and arcs, template and freehand routing, and using the router with a router table. 128 pages.

Router Handbook. With nearly 600 illustrations of every conceivable bit, attachment, jig, and fixture, plus every possible operation, this definitive guide has revolutionized router applications. It begins with safety and maintenance tips, then forges ahead into all aspects of dovetailing, freehanding, advanced duplication, and more. Details for over 50 projects are included. 224 pages.

Router Jigs & Techniques. A practical encyclopedia of information, covering the latest equipment to use with your router, it describes all the newest of commercial routing machines, along with jigs, bits, and other aids and devices. The book not only provides invaluable tips on how to determine the router and bits best suited to your needs, but tells you how to get the most out of your equipment once it is bought. Over 800 photos and illustrations. 384 pages.

Scroll Saw Basics. This overview features more than 275 illustrations covering basic techniques and accessories. Sections include types of saw, features, selection of blades, safety, and how to use patterns. A half-dozen patterns are included to help the scroll saw user get started. Basic cutting techniques are covered including inside cuts, bevel cuts, stack-sawing, and others. 128 pages.

Scroll Saw Handbook. This companion volume to *Scroll Saw Pattern Book* covers the essentials of this versatile tool, including the basics (how scroll saws work, blades to use, etc.) and the advantages and disadvantages of the general types and specific brand-name models available on the market. All cutting techniques are detailed, including compound and bevel sawing, making inlays, reliefs, and recesses, cutting metals and other nonwoods, and marquetry. There's even a section on transferring patterns to wood! Over 500 illustrations. 256 pages.

Scroll Saw Fretwork Patterns. This companion book to *Scroll Saw Fretwork Techniques and Projects* features over 200 fabulous full-size fretwork patterns. These patterns include the most popular classic designs of the past, plus an array of imaginative contemporary ones. Choose from a variety of numbers, signs, brackets, animals, miniatures, and silhouettes, and many more. 256 pages.

Scroll Saw Fretwork Techniques & Projects. This companion book to *Scroll Saw Fretwork Patterns* offers a study in the historical development of fretwork, as well as the tools, techniques, materials, and project styles that have evolved over the past 130 years. Every intricate turn and cut is explained with over 550 step-by-step photos and illustrations. Patterns for all 32 projects are shown in full color. The book also covers some modern scroll-sawing machines and current state-of-the-art fretwork and fine-scroll sawing techniques. 232 pages.

Scroll Saw Pattern Book. This companion book to *Scroll Saw Handbook* contains over 450 workable patterns for making wall plaques, refrigerator magnets, candle holders, pegboards, jewelry, ornaments, shelves, brackets, picture frames, signboards, and many more projects. Beginners and experienced scroll saw users alike will find something to intrigue and challenge them. 256 pages.

Scroll Saw Puzzle Patterns. 80 full-size patterns for jigsaw puzzles, standup puzzles and inlay puzzles. With meticulous attention to detail, Patrick and Patricia Spielman provide instruction and step-by-step photos, along with tips on tools and wood selections, for making standup puzzles in the shape of dinosaurs, camels, hippopotamuses, alligators—even a family of elephants! Inlay puzzle patterns include basic shapes, numbers, an accurate piece-together map of the United States and a host of other colorful educational and enjoyable games for children. 8 pages of color. 256 pages.

Spielman's Original Scroll Saw Patterns. 262 full-size patterns that don't appear elsewhere feature teddy bears, dinosaurs, sports figures, dancers, cowboy cutouts, Christmas ornaments, and dozens more. Fretwork patterns are included for a Viking ship, framed cutouts, wall-hangers, key-chain miniatures, jewelry, self decoration, and much more. Hundreds of step-by-step photos and drawings show how to flop, repeat, and crop each design for thousands of variations. 4 pages of color. 228 pages.

Working Green Wood with PEG. Covers every process for making beautiful, inexpensive projects from green wood without cracking, splitting, or warping. Hundreds of clear photos and drawings show every step from obtaining the raw wood through shaping, treating, and finishing your PEG-treated projects. 175 unusual project ideas. Lists supply sources. 160 pages.

Index